Old Findhorn and Kinloss

Bernard Byrom

In this Edwardian picture the white-painted building in the centre, with steps leading up to a storeroom, is the former Custom House, nowadays called Havenbank. The large gable end of the nearby building is prominent, its sign reading 'Dean's Crown and Anchor Inn and Hiring Establishment', and part of the village's Library and Reading Room is on the right. The white building on the left of the picture is the end of Quay Cottage and the dark-coloured row of houses next to it, on the other side of the main road, are numbered 18, 19 and 21. The left hand doorway has since been replaced by a window so the two houses at that end of the row are now combined into a single one.

© Bernard Byrom, 2022
First published in the United Kingdom, 2022,
by Stenlake Publishing Ltd.
www.stenlake.co.uk
ISBN 978-1-84033-945-1

The publishers regret that they cannot supply copies of any pictures featured in this book.

Printed by
Blissetts, Unit E1-E8 Shield Drive,
West Cross Ind Pk, Brentford, TW8 9EX

Acknowledgements

The author wishes to thank Phil Byrom, Tim Negus, Chairman, Findhorn Village Heritage, and Jim Simpson, Moravia Aerospace Museum, Kinloss, for their assistance during his research for this book.

Further Reading

The books listed below were used by the author during his research. None are available from Stenlake Publishing. Those interested in finding out more are advised to contact their local bookshop or reference library.

Ian K. Dawson: *The Findhorn Railway*
Francis H. Groome: *Ordnance Gazetteer of Scotland 1882*
National Gazetteer of Great Britain and Ireland, 1863
Historic Environment Scotland: historicenvironment.scot
Undiscovered Scotland: undiscoveredscotland.co.uk
The Statistical Accounts of Scotland, 1791-1845
Aberdeen Press & Journal
Elgin Courant and Morayshire Advertiser
Forres, Elgin & Nairn Gazette, Northern Review & Advertiser
Forres News and Advertiser
The Scotsman

The ivy-covered Findhorn House on the left of the picture is nearly 250 years old and nowadays its accommodation is shared between the Royal Findhorn Yacht Club and a luxurious 3-bed apartment for private rent. The gable end of No. 12, Quay Cottage, stands next to it and across the square are the buildings of the former chandlery of James Milne. After his death his daughters gifted it to the village in 1921 to be the village hall and it subsequently became officially the James Milne Institute.

Introduction

The Morayshire village of Findhorn (Gaelic: *Inbhir Eir*) lies on the eastern shore of Findhorn Bay about 25 miles – as the crow flies – east-north-east of Inverness and 5 miles by road from Forres. It is the second village of that name to have been built in the area. Long regarded as the 'Port of Moray', it became a successful international port, but when it was realised that shifting sands had begun to block the harbour and alter the course of the river, a second village and port was built a mile to the south-east. This was a timely move because the old village was subsequently swept away in massive floods on 11 October 1702 when the river burst through to the sea and changed its course.

This second village is the present-day Findhorn, once an important commercial and fishing port. The parish entry in the *New Statistical Account* was written in 1842 and reported that foreign vessels visited the port, sometimes bringing two cargoes yearly of iron, tar and timber from the Baltic, and one of timber from British North America. The articles imported coastwise were barrels of Sunderland and Newcastle coals, lime and coal from the Firth of Forth, slates from Ballachulish, iron from Wales and Staffordshire, salt from Liverpool and bone-dust for manure. Regular trading smacks from London, Leith and Liverpool brought general cargoes of merchandise for Forres, Elgin and Nairn and there were also regular steam vessel services with these places. The produce of the local countryside that was exported consisted of barrels of herrings and salmon, grain of every description, boxes of eggs and loads of timber.

To take advantage of the herring trade, in 1860 a branch railway was opened to Findhorn from a junction with the Inverness & Aberdeen Junction Railway at Kinloss but it was not a commercial success. It closed to passenger traffic after only nine years of operation; goods traffic continued for a while but the rails were lifted and sold in the mid-1870s. The line ran along the quayside as far as the north pier and, to facilitate the loading of ships, a siding was laid on the south pier and accessed via a wagon turntable. A proposal in 1902 to build a light railway to the port came to naught.

An article in the *London Star* newspaper in 1901 described Findhorn as being a village of around 200 houses: "The inhabitants are mostly retired seamen, their widows and men employed at the salmon fisheries – which last, with the letting of lodgings in summer, forms the only industry of the place. Cottages are thatched with 'bent' and whitewashed." The 1911 census recorded a total population of 421 persons, made up of 165 males and 256 females.

The silting up of the harbour and the increasing size of vessels eventually sealed the fate of Findhorn as a trading port. Nowadays it is an attractive village with a lovely bay and superb beach. Extremely popular with summer visitors, it also stages watersports and sailing events.

The village of Kinloss (Gaelic: *Cinn Lois*) is located near the eastern shore of Findhorn Bay about 3 miles south of Findhorn village. Its Cistercian abbey (now a ruin) was founded in 1150 by King David I and went on to become one of the largest and wealthiest religious houses in Scotland. In more recent times an airfield was opened nearby in 1939 and became well-known as RAF Kinloss; the base has since been taken over by the army's 39 Engineer Regiment (Air Support) and is now known as Kinloss Barracks.

The white building in this 1930s view of the centre of the village is the Crown & Anchor Inn. The former Custom House is on the left and the former chandlery owned by James Milne, now the James Milne Institute and with its gable reduced in height, stands in the foreground on the right. The bus standing outside the inn ran a service between the village and Forres. As early as 1907 the following advertisement had appeared in the *Forres News and Advertiser*: "James Dean announces that he will run a BRAKE [a four wheel carriage drawn by two or four horses] twice daily between Findhorn and Forres, leaving Findhorn at 10am and 6.30pm, and returning from Forres at 12.30pm and 7.30pm. Return Fare 1/-.". James Dean operated this bus service until 1949, when it was transferred to Mr. J. Simpson. In 1921 the Morayshire Motor & Engineering Co. Ltd. advertised a motor bus service between Forres and Findhorn three times daily and twice on Sundays for a single fare of 1/-. The Sunday service was increased to three in 1923.

A young family are enjoying themselves in a rowing boat in shallow water near the southern end of the shore, although the weather doesn't look at all like summer and the shingle beach looks as though it must be very painful to the children's bare feet! Moreover, a letter-writer to the *Forres, Elgin & Nairn Gazette* in August 1911 complained about the amount of broken glass bottles strewn on the beach: "I know at any rate the complaints are many and yet the iniquitous habit of throwing broken bottles about to the danger of the public continues, apparently unabated …. having had under my notice two cases of fearfully cut feet resulting from bathing. Anyone who stays at Findhorn must notice how often one sees children going about with bandaged feet." At least today's plastic bottles are less harmful to humans, if more harmful to marine life.

Findhorn harbour is flanked by a pair of parallel piers jutting into the bay. The north pier was constructed in the mid-to-late eighteenth century and the south one, designed by Joseph Mitchell, in 1830. Both piers are constructed of large squares of dressed rubble and topped with the same material. Each pier has two squat *c.*1830 cast-iron bollards. The piers are linked on land with a sloping squared rubble breastwork abutting the shoreline and known as the Loading Bank. In the 1860s the Findhorn Railway's tracks ran along the shore right up to the foot of the north pier which is pictured here. On the right is the Crown Hotel (no longer the Crown & Anchor) and next to it is the former Custom House, now converted into a private residence. The next building is a side view of Harbour House which was built in 1901 and the remaining buildings are the gable ends of the detached house at No. 12, named Quay Cottage, and the terraced houses beyond – Nos. 18, 19 and 21.

The Crown & Anchor Inn dates from 1739 and stands in the centre of the village with its gable standing defiantly against westerly gales. Early nineteenth century photographs show the inn with a thatched roof and with a fine pair of eighteenth-century rusticated ashlar gate piers with ball finials on shaped bases. These flanked the entrance to the present-day outdoor seating area at the front of the inn. It has had many owners and tenants over the years and its woebegone appearance in this picture suggests that it was then awaiting a new owner. The motor car is a Vauxhall Ten 4-door saloon which had a sale price new of £182; this model was built at Luton from 1937-39 and 1946-47, which suggests this photograph was taken in the late 1930s or 1940s.

A group of locals accompanied by a horse-drawn omnibus have gathered in Shore Street in the roadway that has now become the B9011. They are standing outside Station House, the former railway offices and warehouse, which is a two-storey building with attic, with vehicle entry via an archway into a yard. It no longer boasts a porch but in modern times this building has found a new lease of life as the Kimberley House luxury self-catering cottage. Beyond it is the white gable end of the early-mid eighteenth century two-storey five-bay house called Kilravock. The wooden building on the left of the picture with the advertisement for Continental Motor Tyres is the former railway engine shed; next to it is the site of the railway passenger station which was closed in 1869 and later demolished; its site is now marked by a small triangle of grass at the side of the shed. The white building on the right is the Kimberley Inn.

In the nineteenth century and the early years of the twentieth century the bar of the Kimberley Inn was very small and entered through a door from the kitchen. This caused no end of problems with the licensing authorities who were keen to uphold Scotland's draconian Sunday licensing laws that only allowed drinks to be served to *bona fide* travellers, defined as those who had travelled at least three miles. The layout of the building allowed drinkers to claim that they were the guests of the licensee and in 1905 the tenant, Mrs Fraser, was asked to either make a new bar or to separate the bar from the dwelling house.

The southern end of the village, with the tower of the former United Free Church (now the Church of Scotland Kinloss and Findhorn Parish Church) marking the point where the road coming up on the right of the picture from Kinloss divides into two: the Shore Road continuing to the left and the Back Road (High Street) passing behind it through Findhorn village. The large house on the left of the picture is Culbin House, built in 1898, and the white obelisk to the right of the church is the village war memorial which was erected in 1920.

Another view looking south along the shoreline, this time from the 1950s. The boat drawn up on the beach is a coble, designed for salmon fishing. The only signs of life are the man sitting by the wall on the shore and the family of seven who look to be preparing to set off in a rowing boat.

This picture shows 'Bangers' netting salmon at the Culbin Sands sometime around 1920. 'Banging' was the practice of feeding out the nets from the beach in a circular fashion by fishermen in small boats so that the sweep of the encircling nets trapped passing salmon on their way up or downstream. The apparatus on the beach was used to haul in the heavy nets. There was keen rivalry between the various boat crews for the largest catches during the salmon fishing season which was between February and August. The *Old Statistical Account* for the parish of Kinloss, written in 1791, says that "This river abounds with salmon, which, in the spring and beginning of summer, are boiled at Findhorn and kitted and sent to the London market. The only harbour in this parish is Findhorn, which has a bar that is continually changing, and prevents ships of great burden from entering so that trade is carried on in small merchant ships or sloops." Salmon catches diminished during the late twentieth century and the practice ended altogether in 1987. From the late nineteenth century until the early 1960s fish caught in the north-east of Scotland was transported by road to Aberdeen, from where three trains composed exclusively of fish vans left every afternoon in the salmon season. These trains ran to passenger express schedules and were always treated as priority traffic. The fish were packed in ice and arrived fresh at Billingsgate Market before dawn the next morning. This operation is now carried out in purpose-built refrigerated lorries.

A variety of vessels at the north pier, with the Culbin Sands in the background. In the nineteenth century the main imports were such items as merchant goods, sugar, wine, porter and bark, whilst the exports included oats, barley, salmon, linen and yarn. This steam coaster is being unloaded into a rowing boat and the sailing boats at the pier were of the type called Zulus. These were two-masted boats developed for herring fishing and carried three sails (fore, mizzen and jib). The nearest boat bears a Banff registration code.

The Loading Bank, FINDHORN

The land between the two piers and in front of the former Custom House is still known today as the Loading Bank. In days gone by it was used as a transit area for goods ready for loading onto, or having been offloaded from, ships moored at the piers. In this Edwardian picture a shipment of tree trunks is ready for dispatch, watched over by its attendants plus a bevy of onlookers. The Culbin Sands are in the background on the far side of the estuary.

Findhorn Regatta

The annual Findhorn Regatta dates from 1899 and marked the usual end of the salmon fishing season when the fishermen would traditionally celebrate by holding a regatta between the two piers. A typical regatta was reported by the *Forres Elgin & Nairn Gazette* on 23 August 1911 when aquatic sports were held between the two piers. The programme included yacht, yawl, dinghy and coble racing, together with various swimming events, and the Aberdeen Thistle Swimming Club gave exhibitions of swimming, diving, life-saving and water polo. A concert and dance was held in the evening. The event has since expanded into a two-day weekend regatta forming part of Findhorn Week and attracts many holidaymakers to the village as well as many yachtsmen who compete in a variety of races. The buildings in the picture are, from left to right, the Custom House, the Crown & Anchor Inn (note the stylish ashlar entrance pillars to its yard), the hotel stables, and finally the Library and Reading Room, later the James Milne Institute.

In 1921 James Milne's daughters bequeathed his chandlery premises, which were in the centre of the village and close to the south pier, to the village for use as a public hall. This picture dates from the late 1920s after the premises had been partially rebuilt, a clock tower added and the building named the 'James Milne Institute' with the name inscribed in stone above the doorway.

An immense pile of barrels adorn the loading bank in front of the Crown & Anchor Inn and the Custom House in this 1923 picture. The inn's stables are on the other side of the road beyond the entrance pillars. In the days when the bus service to Forres was horse-drawn, several horses were kept here and at the Queens Hotel in Forres to operate the service. James Milne's former chandlery on the right of the picture had only been the village's public hall for about five years at the time of this photograph but already the part of the building on the harbour side had been reduced in height and the ornate clock tower had been added. The details of the buildings are beautifully reflected in the harbour's limpid waters.

This is a view southwards down the B9011 road as it enters Findhorn from Kinloss. The shallow cutting in which the long-closed Findhorn Railway ran is in the forefront of this picture. The marks made by the sleepers can be clearly seen, even though the line had been dismantled many years before this 1910 picture. The cutting was obliterated by the later widening of the road into the village. The villa partly visible on the left is Alma Cottage and beyond it is the single-storey Craigendarroch, followed by Balvenie.

Above: This picture continues in the opposite direction from the one on the facing page and looks towards the road junction where Shore Road continues to the centre of the village and Back Road strikes off to the right. The partly-seen villa on the right of the picture is No. 203 and the next two buildings have nowadays been combined into the single dwelling No. 202 Freedom Cottage. The further of these two buildings was the former Toll House on the Kinloss Road and the windows on each side of its gable were angled so as to give the tollkeeper a clear view along the road in both directions. The former Free Church, with its prominent tower, stands round the corner in Back Road while the unnamed house standing in the fork of the junction is No. 195. Note the narrowness of the road and the unguarded drop into the abandoned railway cutting – driving along that unlit road in the dark must have been extremely hazardous!

Left: This is a closer view of where the B9011 road up from Forres and Kinloss divides into the Shore Road on the left and the Back Road on the right. The latter is the main street through the village and contains the post office and shops; at its far end it curves back to the shore beyond the James Milne Institute in the centre of the village. The nearest house is No. 201, with No. 200 The Retreat beyond it, whilst No. 195 sits in the fork of the junction.

This is a convenient place to introduce the locomotive which ran train services along this short-lived railway. The Findhorn Railway's train services were worked by the Inverness & Aberdeen Railway Company but it had to buy its own locomotive and carriages. Nothing very powerful was needed to work the three-mile branch line and so in 1859 they purchased a small 0-4-0 saddle tank engine, works No. 422, from locomotive builders Neilson & Company of Glasgow. This was one of Neilson's basic designs known as 'Pugs' that they had built throughout the 1850s, primarily for industrial use, and was fitted with rather inefficient Gab motion gear to the wheels and cylinders. It weighed 16 tons, had a boiler working pressure of 120lbs psi, was braked by large wooden blocks acting on the rear of the wheels, had no capacity for carrying coal, and the footplate crew were exposed to the elements.

After the Findhorn Railway closed, the locomotive was purchased by the Inverness & Aberdeen Railway Company in 1862 and became No. 16. This railway became part of the Highland Railway in 1865 and the following year the locomotive was sent to the company's Lochgorm works at Inverness to have its outdated Gab gear replaced with Stephenson Link Motion. At the same time the crosshead boiler feed system and the wheels were also changed. Minor changes included the addition of a tool box on top of the tank and replacement of the old tubular chimney with a more graceful style of capped chimney. After spending some years engaged in shunting duties at Inverness it was sold to Hector Mackenzie of Wick who held the contract for constructing the northernmost section of the Sutherland & Caithness Railway. On completion of the contract the locomotive went south to assist in the construction of the Dunfermline & Queensferry Railway. Its subsequent fate is unknown.

This church, with 650 sittings, was opened on 11 February 1843 as the Free Church of Kinloss by the Rev. Williamson on a site given by H. A. J. Munro of Novar. It stands close to the junction of the Shore Road and Back Road and was built to a design by John Urquhart, a native of Forres (further alterations and repairs were carried out in 1873 by architect John Milne). It is built of coursed rubble granite with ashlar details and surrounds. The doorway has ashlar pillars and pediment and there are double wooden doors with decorative metal hinge plates, whilst the bay is topped by a large rectangular bellcote. The decorative stone finial at the other end of the roof blew down in a gale in 1953 and is now on display inside the church. The largely unchanged interior is a good example of a mid-nineteenth century Free Church. The interior walls are plastered and painted and there are wood-panelled galleries on three sides. These, together with the nave, retain their original pine pews. In 1900 the Free Church united with the United Presbyterian Church and this building became the Findhorn United Free Church. In 1929 the United Free Church denomination united with the Established Presbyterian Church to form the Church of Scotland. The building is now linked with Kinloss as the Church of Scotland Kinloss and Findhorn Parish Church.

Findhorn's war memorial stands opposite the parish church and facing along the main road. The 12-foot-high square obelisk of Kemnay granite was unveiled by Mrs Grant Peterkin of Grange on 14 July 1920 to commemorate those from the parish of Kinloss who died fighting in the First World War. One face is carved with a sheathed cavalry sword with belt attached, whilst below it is a carved laurel wreath with the words "Lest we forget". Twenty-eight names from the First World War are carved on three sides of the obelisk and on the base are the words: "In memory of those brave men from Kinloss Parish who fell in the Great War 1914-1918". Fifteen more names from the Second World War were added in 1948.

Piped water came to the village in 1905/06. In this early twentieth century picture the lady on the left is busy filling her pail at one of the village's public standpipes which stood on the grass triangle on the Back Road in front of Dumella House, watched by three workmen who aren't lifting a finger to help her. The nearest thatched cottage on the right is No. 178, followed by No. 183 Glenmoira. The building further down the same side of the road and jutting into the roadway is No. 143 Tyneholme, with the side of The Neuk peeping out behind it. The thatched building on the near left hand side of the road is a house but isn't numbered on the plan of the village. Beyond it is No. 176 with the two dormers and then the taller house with the window in its gable is No. 161. Much further down the same side of the street is the gable of house No. 127, The Quillet, and next to it is the old bakehouse which stands opposite the present-day post office.

This photograph was taken from near the same spot as the previous picture. The scene is almost identical but the style of the people's clothes and the vehicles dates it to the 1930s. By this time the single-storey No. 143 Tyneholme in the distance has been fitted with a dormer window. A solitary paraffin lamp standard is on the right but with an empty holder; electricity came to the village in 1936 so maybe the lamp was in the process of being converted or removed.

This picture shows the deplorable state of the Back Road (aka High Street) around the turn of the twentieth century, looking from the village centre towards ivy-clad Dumella House in the distance. The confectionery and stationery shop on the left, owned by Mrs M. Robertson, was called The Neuk. The shop has, alas, been long demolished but the white gabled building next door, No. 143 Tyneholme, still stands with its thatched roof now slated. The building with dormers across the road is No. 142 Bon Accord and next to it was the then post office, whilst the house beyond with the porch was the village's poor house. Notice the public water standpipe behind the little girl's head.

This scene is a little further down Back Road, still looking towards Dumella House. Groups of children are standing or sitting around near the public water standpipe, enjoying the afternoon sunshine while a delivery man goes on his rounds with his pony and cart. Notice that one of the three girls on the left has brought her pail to draw water from the standpipe. The single-storey thatched house on the left, No. 160, now has a slated roof with dormers while the house opposite, No. 161, looks virtually unchanged today.

This view looks in the opposite direction to the previous pictures, along the Back Road towards a throng of smartly-dressed Edwardian children who are making way for a tradesman's horse-drawn cart. The building on the left, No. 127, is called The Quillet and next to it is the shop of 'Issy' Dey, whose sign above the door proclaims her to be a baker and confectioner as well as selling refreshments. The villa across the road, substantially remodelled, is now the village post office. Many of the other buildings in the picture have either been substantially modified or demolished to allow for road widening.

An Edwardian view of Findhorn, looking southwards down the beach with a three-masted schooner berthed at the north pier. The small white fishing boat on the shingle displays 'INS 562', denoting its registration as being at Inverness, and the wooden beams on the left were racks on which fishing nets were dried. The white-painted salmon fishermen's bothies on the left stand next to their manager's house, then comes ivy-covered Findhorn House; next is the village Reading Room and Library and beyond it, stretching southwards, is a panorama of the whole shoreline of the village

In this scene from the early years of the twentieth century the loading bank is in the foreground, leading up to the Custom House. The white building in the centre is Quay Cottage and the large building on its left is Findhorn House, built in 1775. Today the nearer section of this house, with its gables facing the harbour, contains a luxury ground floor apartment whilst the remainder of the building is the headquarters of the Royal Findhorn Yacht Club.

The Findhorn Yacht Club was founded in 1929 with James Chadwick as its first Commodore and used his home, Findhorn House (pictured here), as its premises. This impressive building, built in the late eighteenth century and with nineteenth-century additions, eventually ended up as its clubhouse and headquarters. The yacht club was awarded its Royal title in 1971.

Cleveland House stands on the B9011 road beyond the yacht club; it is now called The Haven and is completely enclosed by its white wall. The railings and gate have gone and, more significantly, so has the stone porch with its decorated top. In its place is a stone and glass conservatory that stretches across the whole width of the frontage, making its present-day appearance almost unrecognisable from this picture. The women on the right are standing in Caledon Place where the walls of the two-storey house have since been rendered and the smaller house beyond it, which appears to have a thatched roof, has had a second storey added to make it the same height as the first house.

Today, a larger car park is situated near where these holidaymakers are parked, which is a short distance north of the village at the beginning of an area of sand dunes. The makes and models of the motor cars place the scene firmly in the mid-1950s. The house on the left of the picture is Sandspoint and the large white building next to it is the Culbin Sands Hotel.

The Back Shore, FINDHORN

The Back Shore at Findhorn is the portion of the shore that faces northwards onto the Moray Firth. These Edwardian ladies relaxing on the shore, complete with baby and pram, look incongruous among the Findhorn salmon fishermen who are drying and cleaning their nets. The nets were usually first covered with sand, then hung up to dry. The sand helped to dry out the seaweed that had become attached to the nets, then it was beaten off with home-made switches. It may have been a relaxing occasion for the ladies but that would not be a reason for them to remove their hats in public.

The Back Shore, to the north of the village beyond the sand dunes, is a mixture of sand and shingle. This 1950s picture shows holidaymakers doggedly spending time on the beach on what is obviously a cold day, judging from the fact that almost everyone is fully dressed. The sea looks decidedly rough; only a few hardy bathers are around, and the ice cream vendor is probably wishing he was selling hot dogs instead! Salmon fishermen's nets can be seen floating in the white surf, ready to trap unwary salmon making their way up or down the estuary.

Beach huts have been a prominent feature on Findhorn's beaches since the early 1930s when they were advertised in the *Forres News & Advertiser* as "Standard 8 x 6 x 6 foot complete with cupboard, fold-down table and form, erected on site for £7.10s." New ones have been added in recent years with a price tag of £25,000 for a 54 square-feet hut! In this picture holidaymakers are enjoying the sunshine on a more shingly part of the Back Shore and are looking out over the Moray Firth.

This picture shows the back of the village in 1904, with sand dunes right up to the buildings. In 1926 this land formed part of a 9-hole par 36 golf course designed by Andrew Phimister of Grantown-on-Spey for the Findhorn Golf Club. Membership peaked at 80 in the mid-1930s but the Second World War brought devastation to the course because it was commandeered for military training purposes. Post-war attempts to revive the club met with little success; it finally ceased to function in 1954 and the foreground in the picture is today occupied by the Findhorn Sands Holiday Park, and static caravans have replaced the dunes.

The substantial Victorian stone residence of Cullerne House, nowadays known as Mount Villa, lies on the southern outskirts of Findhorn, off the B9011 on the way to Kinloss. Its main entrance is accessed through stone gate posts with large iron gates and along a tree-lined driveway. In April 1947 it was reported in the *Aberdeen Press & Journal* that "Cullerne House has been sold privately by Mr Christie Anderson, Forres, to Lord Malcolm Douglas-Hamilton, brother of the Duke of Hamilton". The house possesses 6 bedrooms, 3 reception rooms and 3 bathrooms, spacious high-ceiling rooms, wooden sash and case windows, and various ornate features. Its latest sale was in 2022, after having been placed on the market with offers invited of over £650,000.

The Culbin Sands stretch along the coast from Findhorn Bay in the east down to Nairn in the west. This was once an area of 4,000 acres of fertile agricultural land that supported a thriving crofting and farming community. The nearby sand dunes were thick with marram grass (pictured here) which bound the dunes together but centuries of deforestation and uprooting of the grass for thatching houses led to the land being destabilised. This resulted in several sandstorms arising during gales, the ultimate one being in 1694 when the land and the villages in the area were finally buried beneath the sand and abandoned. The dunes are seen here in 1936 and were once the largest expanse of loose dune sand desert in Britain. In 1922 the Forestry Commission began a forty year programme of planting the dunes with pine trees to stabilise them; the result is today's huge Culbin Forest which, together with the remaining sands, is famous for its walks and variety of wildlife.

The Bay Hotel was designed by architect Charles Doig of Elgin and built by Alexander Edward of Sanquhar, who had already built the Moray Arms in Forres. It opened on 6 June 1903 and the *Elgin Courant and Morayshire Advertiser* reported that the "Ground floor has drawing and smoking rooms, parlour and bar whilst on the second floor, which is approached by a very wide staircase, there are drawing and dining rooms plus bedrooms and bathrooms and on the second floor are more bedrooms and bathrooms". The hotel initially had a chequered career. The first licensee was John Chisholm of the Station Hotel Refreshment Rooms, Keith, but he didn't stay very long; William Donaldson entered as tenant in May 1904 but was examined in bankruptcy in February 1907, explaining that the hotel had failed because of want of business, the season lasting only about 8 weeks. The Craigellachie Brewery Company Ltd then became the landlord but that too went into liquidation in 1907! The hotel was put up for sale but wasn't sold until 1911. The following advertisement appeared in the *Forres News & Advertiser* of 24 June 1911: "Now open for season, under entirely new management. Modern and up-to-date in every respect. Bathrooms and Hot and Cold water on every floor. Tariff: May £1.5s per person per week, July £1.15s or 4/6 per day per person." Business must have settled down for a few years because the next notice that can be found in the local press announced in January 1924 that the hotel was "To be let, furnished, on a lease. 4 public rooms, private parlour, 13 bedrooms, other usual accommodation, garage. Gravitation, water supply with sewerage connection to the sea." This last facility wouldn't be much of an attraction to today's holidaymakers!

Major Thomas A. Ross MC DCM acquired the Bay Hotel in 1925 after a distinguished military career. He announced his intention that in future the hotel would be known as the Culbin Sands Hotel. However, he sold the hotel in 1929 to Andrew Cruickshank of Grantown-on-Spey who died suddenly in 1932. Fast forward to September 1948 when the hotel was again on the market, advertised in *The Scotsman* as having a "lounge, dining room, conservatory facing sea, private room, public bar and sitting room, 14 bedrooms, 2 bathrooms, 4 lavatories, kitchen, scullery, pantry, larders etc., 6 lockup garages." Nothing more is found in the local papers until 1970 when the hotel was bought by John D. McLennan, a former paratrooper, who also took over the nearby house, *Sandspoint*, to provide extra accommodation. During the two years he owned the hotel he introduced cabaret and striptease shows, and complaints were raised because even if a person only wanted a drink, 3/- was charged to enter the lounge when the cabaret was there. The next owner of the Culbin Sands Hotel, Mr Iain Fergusson, said in 1972 that he hoped to run a family-type hotel and would not continue late-night cabaret and strip shows. Mr Fergusson ran the hotel for three years, then it changed hands at least once more before it was finally bought in 1988 by Mr and Mrs Findlay McNaughton. Its time as a hotel was fast running out as the *Aberdeen Press & Journal* reported on 3 December 1993: "An ambitious £1 million residential development is envisaged for the Moray holiday and yachting resort of Findhorn. The scheme will involve the demolition of the seafront Culbin Sands Hotel to make way for the construction of 27 two-bedroom luxury flats." This duly happened and today no trace remains of this once-popular hotel.

These static caravans in 1962 were the beginning of today's Findhorn Bay Holiday Park at the southern end of the village overlooking RAF Kinloss. The conditions look very primitive compared with today's facilities at the site, especially looking at the laundry blowing in a stiff westerly wind – will it survive the holiday or will it end up a few miles away in Elgin?

Kinloss parish church was originally built in 1765 and incorporates some of the foundations of an earlier seventeenth-century church built after the parish of Kinloss was formed in 1657. It has seen numerous later extensions and alterations. William Robertson of Elgin rebuilt the south wall and added new windows in 1830, Alexander Urquhart built the north aisle in 1834, and A & W Reid, architects, built the east tower in 1863. Finally, the organ was built by Harrison & Harrison of Durham and installed in 1879. The church is mainly rubble built and harled, although the tower at the east end is built in roughly-tooled and shaped sandstone and all the windows and doorways have ashlar surrounds. The square tower is centrally placed against the east gable of the nave and has two main stages, topped by a corbelled and battlemented parapet built in ashlar stone. The interior walls are plastered and painted and the wooden beam roof structure is exposed and supported by corbels in the walls. The nave has a small gallery at the east end, accessed by spiral stairs in the tower. The gallery retains its simple wooden pews, in front of which are box pews with little doors, very likely reserved for important or wealthy local families in the past. The interior of the church has been modified several times during its history, the latest change being the replacement of the downstairs pews by stackable chairs.

Kinloss Abbey, which was founded in 1150 by King David I and dedicated to St Mary, was first occupied by Cistercian monks from Melrose Abbey. It received its Papal Bull from Pope Alexander III in 1174 and later came under the protection of the Bishop of Moray in 1187. The abbey went on to become one of the largest and wealthiest religious houses in Scotland, receiving the valuable salmon fishing rights on the River Findhorn from Robert the Bruce in 1312; rights that were subsequently renewed by James I and James IV. The buildings were greatly extended in the 1530s. During its history the abbey received many royal visitors including Edward I in 1303, Edward III in 1336 and Mary, Queen of Scots in 1562. The abbey had 24 abbots in all, the most famous being Robert Reid who was appointed in 1528 and rose to become Bishop of Orkney and eventually Lord President of the Court of Session, which is the head of the judiciary in Scotland. On his death in 1558 he left significant funds for the founding of a seat of learning in Edinburgh and these formed the basis of the endowment of the University of Edinburgh when it was established by Royal Charter in 1582.

The Reformation in Scotland of 1560 did not bring about the immediate demise of the abbey. Over the years that followed its lands and properties were gradually run down and in 1601 what was left was granted to Edward, Lord Bruce of Kinloss. The abbey building itself was sold to Alexander Brodie of Lethen in 1643 and in 1652 he sold most of its stones to Oliver Cromwell's army for use in the building of their citadel at Inverness. The graveyard is still used as a burial ground today.

These four conjoined thatched cottages on the B9011 road to Findhorn at its junction with the B9089 road to Burghead represent almost the whole of the old village of Kinloss. Today the nearest cottage is still residential, being the proprietors' accommodation, because the next two cottages have been transformed into the Abbey Inn. The fourth cottage, here sporting a newly-slated roof, is currently the Kinloss Chinese Takeaway. The tower of Kinloss and Findhorn Parish Church can be discerned through the trees beyond the cottages. Note the public water standpipe on the corner and the two paraffin street lamps.

The former Royal Air Force station at Kinloss opened on 1 April 1939 and served as a night bomber crew training establishment during the Second World War. A wide variety of aircraft used the station during the war; the grass runways were enlarged and paved, and two secondary runways were constructed. After the war it was handed over to Coastal Command to monitor Russian ships and submarines in the Norwegian sea. Until 2010 it was the main base for the RAF's fleet of Hawker Siddeley Nimrod MR2 maritime patrol aircraft which also engaged in Search and Rescue missions. These aircraft were meant to be retired in 2010 and replaced with BAE Nimrod MRA4 aircraft but, when plans for the latter were cancelled, Kinloss station became surplus to RAF requirements. Its equipment and personnel were replaced in 2012 by the army's 39 Engineer Regiment (Air Support) and it is nowadays known as Kinloss Barracks.

A line-up of Nimrod MR2 aircraft at Kinloss airfield, standing on the main parking apron in front of the floodlights which were used at night time and during poor weather operations. The aircraft was developed from the De Haviland Comet 4, the world's first pressurised jet airliner, and was designed by Hawker Siddeley with further development by British Aerospace and BAE Systems. It was equipped with 4 Rolls-Royce Spey engines and had a maximum speed of 925 kph. Two prototypes were built, followed by 49 production aircraft. Kinloss was the main base for these marine patrol aircraft which first flew in May 1967 and were retired in June 2011. During the Cold War they monitored Russian ships and submarines in the Norwegian Sea and were equipped with nuclear depth charges. A Nimrod (named *Duke of Edinburgh*) has been preserved on the airfield and another at the Yorkshire Air Museum at Elvington, near York.